Light Codes for the Soul

Wisdom, Symbols, and Stories for Energy Healing and Ascension

Light Codes for the Soul

Wisdom, Symbols, and Stories for Energy Healing and Ascension

by

Laara

Copyright Notice

Publisher: Peacock Wisdom Publishing

ISBN (Paperback): 978-1-7773515-0-2
ISBN (Hardcover): 978-1-7773515-2-6
ISBN (eBook): 978-1-7773515-1-9

WAIVER: The author of this book does not dispense medical advice or other professional advice or prescribe the use of any technique as a form of diagnosis or treatment for any physical, emotional, or medical condition. The intent of the author is only to offer information of an anecdotal and general nature that may be part of your quest for emotional and spiritual wellbeing. In the event that you or others use any of the information or other content in this book, the author and the publisher assume no responsibility for the direct or indirect consequences. The reader should consult his or her medical, health, or other professional before adopting any of the suggestions in this book or drawing inferences from it.

This book is dedicated to every eternal being
choosing to embrace Love and Light.
May you know your true self in accordance with the
Love That You Are.

Acknowledgments

Thank you to all who have encouraged me to share these special messages. I feel truly blessed to have the opportunity, support, and guidance to bring forward the sacred energies of Light Language in written form.

To my parents, Chuck and Alison Herod, you have provided me with every opportunity possible in loving support of my journey. I am eternally grateful for the roles you have played in my life, and for your openness in accepting me and allowing me the freedom to follow my heart's callings.

To my wonderful teachers, Rosalyn L. Bruyere, Ken Weintrub, and Dr. Stewart Blaikie, I am grateful for your healings, and for your assistance as I offer healings to those who find this book. To my Guides: Master Ling, Lady Isis, and Jeshua, and all of the Light Beings who support the healing and advancement on Gaia, my deepest Love and gratitude.

To Kristen Wise, Dawn Bassick, Maíra Pedreira, Karen Whiteside, and Ben Lott, thank you for your amazing professionalism, and for your assistance in producing and supporting the development of my work.

To Michael Ireland, my dear editor. Thank you for keeping intact the integrity of the voice of Spirit that speaks through these channeled messages. You are a special gift to the world of publishing.

To my dear readers … thank you for your continued support. I am honored to be able to share these sacred and healing messages with you.

—*Laara*

Contents

Illustrations

PREFACE

In the spring of 2020, the world was turning upside down. There was chaos, confusion, suffering on all levels, and people were fearing what the future would bring. I was on a two-week, self-isolation quarantine after arriving back home to Canada from a book tour in Australia and New Zealand. It was a stark contrast coming home after such a wonderful trip, as my partner and I arrived to a completely different world than the one we had left.

I realized then that as a collective, humanity had taken its dysfunction to a new level, which is a common occurrence during a transition of Ages. As we let go of the Piscean Age, and learn to embrace the Age of Aquarius, some bumps are to be expected. We have entered the Age of Purification and there is now an important purging of low vibratory energies. Humanity is receiving an influx of new, high vibratory frequencies, both man-made and outer-worldly, and the lower vibrational energies are surfacing to be seen. This unfolding is an important process as we set our sights on the Golden Age, creating Heaven on Earth.

Each of us as individuals faces a choice: remain unaware ("asleep" as spiritual people say), or "wake up" and embrace the truths arising within us. Fortunately, as we embrace the higher vibrations, we receive wonderful downloads and upgrades of our gifts and talents—and as a collective, we contribute to the healing of our beloved planet. It is a unique and special time to be incarnated on Gaia.

While I was in quarantine after arriving home, I decided to give myself the gift of experiencing a personal Vipassana spiritual retreat. I turned off my phone, didn't speak with anyone—and dove inward. I meditated, practiced yoga, went for walks in the forest and on the beach, and even swam in the chilly Pacific Ocean (the ocean is cold in Canada!). During my retreat, I received a massive download. I had begun working on a book— my second on Light Codes—which was meant to provide wisdom and insight in support of the physical body. But it seems that *that book* wasn't the one I was meant to focus on, because the download I received—almost in its entirety—was *this* book.

The message that I received (in a nutshell) is that humanity is in need of healing at the very core. To heal our wounds we need to cut to the chase; we need to understand *why* we experience any upset energies at all. What a gift it would be if we were all able to release our suffering. Just imagine what it would be like: No pain. No suffering. No needs. In our essence, we are energetically full, stable, strong, and capable. This is our truth. This is our Love. Anything outside of this is false, and it is this falseness that is in need of healing.

My wish for you, dear reader, is that you skip through this book as your intuition guides you. Trust yourself. Everything you need is within you. This book is simply a reminder of what's already there. Use what resonates with you, discard what doesn't, and combine other modes of healing to supplement your journey back to the Love That You Are. No one thing or action is a cure for this tangled mess we are in … but remember … there are no limitations! That being said, the holistic approach is always wisest.

All blessings, dear souls. Thank you for being here at this time. You are needed, you have been called. You are greeted with open arms and all my Love.

Laara
Victoria, B.C.

Chapter 1

Introduction

The Way of the Codes

Many of us have common goals that we desire to fulfill in our lifetimes. We accumulate mental checklists: We want to be happy and healthy, we want a job we enjoy and are good at, we want a partner who loves us, maybe we even want to have a family. We want to have friends and a social life, to live in a certain place, to acquire special trinkets and toys … and we want to make enough money, feel powerful, and be respected and appreciated by others.

Maybe we attain some of our goals. One by one, we check them off of our mental list, and we take note of how long it took us to move up our inner achievement ladder. Some things in our life feel perfect and some things are close to perfect. Then there are the things that are not perfect. Do those count? With all of the perfect things and the imperfect things, how do we feel? Do we feel complete? Truly happy? Full of Love and joy?

How much of our lives do we spend searching, consciously or unconsciously, for the next thing on our list in order to fill a void deep within our being? How much of our lives do we spend dissatisfied because we haven't achieved some of the things others in our tribe have been successful in acquiring?

We find that we are searching for something … something to fill the emptiness. Maybe we turn to spirituality. Maybe we learn about different psychological techniques or energy healing techniques and we set out to uncover pieces of ourselves that we aren't so sure we want to uncover. "Some things are better left alone," we think. So, we get caught in a never-ending cycle. We search our hearts, we get scared, we jump into addictions and bad habits, then we hurl abuse at ourselves (and others), all the while struggling, hoping to find a way to cure our "deficiency." And maybe (if we're lucky) we discover that our less-than-desirable tendencies, behaviors, and personality traits—about which we judge ourselves—are the wounds of our inner child.

Once the wounded child within us reveals itself and we grasp the confusion, pain, and suffering this aspect of us holds, we can become overwhelmed as we process the intense emotions, sensations, and longings that arise. We might look for outlets to soothe our inner child, to satisfy its wants and desires. *How can we make sense of what is surfacing?* Perhaps we feel vulnerable and sensitive. Perhaps we feel anger and frustration. *Have we always felt this way?*

Next logical step: Google it. We discover fun quizzes and articles describing Highly Sensitive People, Empathic People, Indigo Children, Crystal Children, Twin Flames ... the list goes on. We are in heaven! "I'm different and special!" our inner child exclaims as we search each social media platform. We study what it means to be all of these things ... we get distracted for a little while ... until one day, we realize that our wonderful exploration of self-discovery was simply one more step on our journey towards self-mastery.

The more we search and discover, the more questions arise. The questions lead to more searching, more discovery. We go on a shopping spree, ordering incense, candles, tarot cards, oracle cards, multiple spiritual books, posters, and of course, crystals. We play with our spiritual toys for a while, yet we continue to bump along on our journey no matter how many essential oils we buy! We find ourselves still dissatisfied. We might contemplate and engage with the pressures of time ... we feel that we are "behind" somehow, that we need to "catch up." As we expand our awareness of the physical, mundane three-dimensional realm, our vibrations increase, which fuels the purging of lower vibrational energies. We feel our souls kicking into higher gear and now we want to connect with our spirit guides and the Ascended Masters. We pursue initiation into healing modalities and higher consciousness and we rejoice as each stage of our journey unfolds.

But still ... the void lingers.

The void we feel is our disconnection from our Love. It is the disconnection from our higher self, soul, and Source energy. This book will attempt to show you the story behind this disconnection, so you may find your way back home.

The Purpose of this Book

The purpose of this book is to help you reconnect to your soul: the divine, sublime you, who is fully connected to All That Is. This book has been written to help you to tap into your individual truth, so that you may see with clarity the stories that shape and color your life. It is to provide you with an opportunity to heal, once and for all, the great wound which sparked the fire of your pain, suffering, and confusion. It is to empower you and offer you a roadmap back to your true self. It is a gift you give yourself which can help you to find that "something" that until now you could never seem to find. The purpose of this book is to show you the way home: back to the energy that feeds your soul. How you name this energy, God, Source, Divine, Universe (or any name you connect with) is up to you. The workings of the energy remain stable in any name of the Light that resonates with your heart. For the purposes of this book, we will refer to this ultimate energy as "Love" and as "Source."

What Are Light Codes?

Everything is energy. Look around at the space you are in. Everything you see (and everything you can't see), at a fundamental level, is energy. Energy is Light. Light holds all of the information in existence, on all levels of existence. Information is knowledge, wisdom, and everything consciously known and unknown. Information is actualized through consciousness—and consciousness arises when energy (Light) is focused into a point of awareness. Our individual consciousness, although existing with infinite expansion, is limited by our scope of awareness. It is our awareness that is limiting, and it is our expanded consciousness that is called upon to help increase our awareness beyond our physical, three-dimensional senses and experiences.

Light Language transcends human language, because our limited languages cannot describe the mechanics of the universe. Human language doesn't have the expansiveness of Light Language, but even so, our spoken word carries energy. Our words are important, the way in which we speak them is important. Our words are an expression of our Love, and they have a direct impact on our manifested reality.

Light Language is the conscious tuning into and expressing of a massive, multidimensional stream of information. This expression can be literally anything. Light Language is expressed through everything in nature, and nature is everything in the universe that is in accordance with Love. Human beings are an expression of Light Language. A flower blooming, a bird singing, ocean waves crashing upon a shoreline, sun glistening off a lake—anything that makes your heart feel warm is Light Language. Art is an expression of Light Language, as are dance, music, and photography. Mathematics and science are types of Light Language too. Light Language flows within and around all things, it is part of the expression and creation of all things.

The Stream of Energy

The universe provides a multitude of options for us as human beings to connect to the infinite information and energies that feed and nourish us. When I write or sign

Light Language, I am consciously tuning into the Light stream of infinite information—condensing this information into little symbols and squiggles—while keeping the integrity of the energetic message intact. I access this stream of energy through the chakras above the crown, including my heart, third eye, and crown chakras. But in order to channel it effectively onto this plane, I remain grounded and present in my body. I raise my vibration, and because I am adept at it now, I connect to the energy instantly. It's like hooking myself up to a jet stream of energetic information. I hold a topic in mind and allow my expanded consciousness to call upon the information and to assemble and actualize it into a single point of awareness within my being. Once this has occurred (it is instantaneous), I can speak, write, or sign this information in the form of Light Language or Light Codes.

The Difference Between Light Language and a Light Code

Light Language is the expression of the infinite, multidimensional knowledge, wisdom, and information stored in Light. When we condense Light Language (in the same way we might condense a computer file so it's easier to store, export, or import), we get a Light Code. Because of their condensed nature, for some, Light Codes can be easier to work with than Light Language. Rather than concentrating on a longer expression (as is seen with traditional Light Language), we can focus on a single symbol or image, which holds within it a vast, complex, multi-layered message from the universe. Light Codes are immeasurably helpful and supportive to humanity and to the collective consciousness of all souls. Some of their benefits include:

- Activating our energetic bodies
- Turning on dormant DNA and RNA
- Acting like missing puzzle pieces for healing and ascension
- Serving as methods for our soul, spiritual guidance, and Source energy to get a message to our subconscious or conscious mind
- Helping to strengthen specific levels of our beings (including our mental/emotional/physical/ spiritual aspects)
- Helping us to expand our consciousness and develop our mental/emotional/physical/spiritual awareness
- Triggering change in alignment with our soul
- Opening and connecting chakras and meridians
- Working with all levels of our being
- Healing present, past, and ancestral; global, inter-dimensional, and intergalactic levels of being
- Being comforting and relatable
- Serving as methods of connecting with the soul, the higher self, and the Spirit
- Serving as ways for Spirit to communicate with us.

Light Codes are available to anyone, are safe for everyone to use, and also serve as:

- ☺ Communication healing tools
- ☺ Maps to a higher function of expression
- ☺ Visual homeopathies
- ☺ Technologies for communicating with the conscious, subconscious, super subconscious, and superconscious minds
- ☺ Multidimensional frequencies connecting with you wherever you are along your journey
- ☺ Expressions of purity, Love, creation, and truth
- ☺ The language of the universe—the universal language recognized by our soul.

Raise your Vibration (Fill Your Body with Light)
Each time you practice with Light Codes or read stories about them, take your time to contemplate their wisdom. I recommend that you use the grounding technique below to help facilitate an optimal, receptive energetic state of being, so you can work with the Light Codes as consciously as possible. This exercise engages the minor chakras on the bottoms of your feet to help you to ground, center, and attune with the vibrational frequency of the information, stories, and Light Codes provided in this book.

Grounding Practice Meditation
Sit in a chair with your feet flat on the floor. Relax. Breathe
slowly. On each inhale, imagine that your feet are suction
cups, pulling energy up from the earth. On each exhale,
relax. With each inhale, imagine your feet pulling energy up
from the earth, through the floor, into your legs. Feel the
energy moving up within your body with each in-breath,
until it reaches the top of your head. Release it out of
the top of your head (your crown chakra). Imagine the
energy flowing out like a waterfall. Practice this grounding
exercise often, so it becomes second nature. Using this
process at the beginning of your meditation practice will
help center you and prepare you to enter any level of
awareness you may wish to access. Grounding connects
your heart and mind. It can promote wellness, improve
sleep, lower your blood pressure, and reduce stress and
anxiety—it's a great way to start and end each day!

Clarification of Terms:

Light and Love and "Light" vs. "light"
When Light is described in this book, we are referring to
Divine Light. Divine Light is the Light of "All That Is"—
Source energy or Universal energy. It is God's Light, it is
your infinite Light. Your Light is the Love That You Are.

"Love" vs. "love"

Love as an action ("loving" or "to love") is different than the Love That You Are (your true, authentic self). We capitalize Love throughout this book when we are referring to the truth of who you are, to your essence or Soul Light, as well as to Universal/Source/God Love.

On Time

Time is a distinctive carrier band, similar to that of a radio wave of energy. There are multiple frequencies (carrier bands) of time, and depending on our individual resonance, we find an energetic connection to a particular line or frequency of time. Our resonance depends upon our soul's mission, our karma, or simply our individual frequency.

Time is an unfixed, four-dimensional construct, which has an effect within the third dimension. Time moves in a spiral, providing us with an opportunity to revisit the "past" in the "future." There are multiple timelines active on this planet "at this time." We are even able to switch timelines in our lifetimes. The person you pass on the street may be experiencing a very different life than yours, and could even be living on a different timeline. Because of the unfixed nature of time, everyone experiences time differently.

How to Use this Book

In this book, the Light Codes are not arranged in any particular order. Their sequence within these pages is not significant. You may choose to read this book cover to cover, or you are welcome to choose a symbol that resonates with you at any time. You may enjoy taking a few moments to breathe with the Grounding Practice provided, and then when you are ready, asking the universe to show you which page is most appropriate for you on this day. Then pick up the book and allow a page to open before you. Or, perhaps you want to flip through the pages to a symbol you are drawn to—and work with that symbol as long as you feel is necessary.

Reading this book is an exercise in reclaiming your power, authenticity, and truth. The channeled messages and wisdom woven through its pages will assist you in connecting more deeply with The Ultimate Divine Energies, understanding them, and correcting any misconceptions you may have about them. Many of these Light Codes have short descriptions accompanying them, but note: These descriptions are intended only for the purpose of conscious identification. In some cases, explanatory text accompanies a Code. As noted earlier, while Light Code messages transcend human language, sometimes, by knowing on a conscious level what a sigil represents, we can engage with that Light Code with more authority and awareness. Sometimes, however, the Codes stand alone, affording you space and freedom to connect with their energies without the imposition or limitation of language. Their infinite knowledge and wisdom speak directly to your energy body, your heart, your higher self, and your soul. What better way to do soul healing than by using a language that your soul and higher self recognize and speak?

You may be surprised by the messages of the channeled stories or amazed by the energies the symbols emit. Conversely, some may disturb you. Whatever occurs as you interact with each symbol, know that your reactions are normal. Be patient and gentle with yourself. Just observe your responses. There is no rush. Take as much time as you need to reflect on each Code. You can even postpone working with a particular story or Light Code. Often our reactions will trigger a memory or lead us into a specific area that needs healing. By focusing on the issues we are guided to, we can tackle deeper wounds. You can always circle back!

Working with the Messages and Light Codes

Although these messages are channeled, we are each still limited by our personal language and our individual history. Therefore, as you read the messages and stories you must apply your own interpretation. For example, as you read, you may begin to ponder your own life story. How has your life been shaped, directed, or defined by the wounds of your soul? We encourage you to meditate upon and contemplate the messages in this book and in the process, to allow your own truth to emerge. Allow your mind to consider multiple viewpoints for any Code, story, or message—what do they mean in the context of who you are and who you want to become?

Meditating

We invite you to use the Grounding Practice Meditation provided as a baseline practice for working with Light Codes. The meditation will help you to become present, grounded, relaxed, and open to receive the messages and energies on a more conscious level. Or, you may find that your own favorite meditations help to bring you into a grounded state of being—so use those instead. As with all things, the more conscious we are, the more connected and empowered we are and the more meditation both expands our conscious mind and helps us to tap into the collective unconscious. That said, Light Codes work with us for our highest good, whether we are aware of them or not. (Note: If you wish to take the messages provided in this book to a deeper place in the Quantum Field, we recommend checking out Fractalline Healing™.)

Using Affirmations

Throughout this book, you will find helpful affirmations. Affirmations can be powerful tools in gaining clarity of mind and focusing your energy toward a desired outcome. As with everything within this book, take what resonates; leave what doesn't behind. Feel free to alter the language of the affirmations to suit your needs. Please read the guidelines for Intention-Setting below to assist you in amplifying the manifestation qualities of the affirmations.

Suggestions for Working with Light Codes

Intention-Setting

We are thinking, feeling, conscious, creative human beings with the capacity to make what we think become our reality. When we intend to manifest certain things in our lives, it is important to be clear, specific, and detailed in our intentions *and* to engage with our physical senses as we hold an intention in our conscious minds. In order for our intentions to have momentum, we must engage at least two (and preferably more) of our physical senses simultaneously. We must see, hear, feel, smell, and even taste the thing we intend to create. The more senses we can engage, the more real our intention becomes and the more likely it is to manifest in physical form.

So, we need to *choose* (as our act of intention-setting) to work with these symbols in an honorable way, bringing forth our most excellent selves to the best of our ability. Remember, there is no pressure, just do your best to accept yourself for who you are and where you are on any given day. Showing up is half the battle. When you work with a symbol, be clear in your intention that you are choosing to heal that which no longer serves you, and that you are making room within your being for more Love, happiness, health, and abundance!

Tracing

Trace the Light Codes on a piece of paper—create your own unique art. Make each one special, and place it in a suitable location. Hang it on your wall, set it on your night stand, or make it a special feature of your altar. It can also be helpful to carry with you the Light Code that is resonating for you at any given time. Keep it in your wallet, purse, or pocket.

Working with Crystals

You may want to charge a crystal with the energies emitted by any Light Code. Begin by clearing any lower vibrational energy from the crystal by using salt water, sunlight, or smudge (what you use depends on the composition of the crystal). Research the best way to clear and cleanse your crystal, as some will dissolve in salt water or fade in sunlight.

Once your crystal is clear, place it on top of the Light Code you wish to work with. Ask the Beings of Love and Light, your crystal, and the symbol itself to assist you in transferring the energy from the Light Code into your crystal, in the Highest Good for All. How long should you leave the crystal and Light Code together? Trust your intuition (or your gut feelings). You might feel that the energy transfers happen instantly or that it's best to leave them together overnight.

There is no right or wrong way to work with Light Codes. Allow yourself the freedom of self-discovery. As we are all evolving continuously, our needs change. Give yourself permission to change how you work with and interact with these sacred symbols. Follow your inner guidance and you will get the most out of the Light Codes—what feels most in alignment with you?

Chapter 2

Soul Connection

Conscious Connection to the Soul

Conscious Connection to the Soul

This Code reminds us that we are always connected to our soul in wonderful and mysterious ways—and that we are all capable of connecting to this higher aspect of the Self. As you tune into the frequencies of this symbol, let go of any notions you might hold of what it is like to connect with your soul. There's nothing to do but breathe. Allow your experience to be what it is.

Relax. Try using the grounding meditation provided in the beginning of the book. When you feel ready, gaze upon the sigil in your perfect timing, keeping your mind as relaxed as possible. Feel into whatever arises for you.

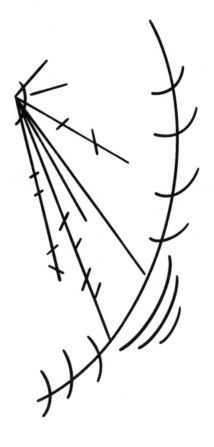

Soular Wound

Soular Wound

This is a Light Code representing the "soular wound." When we connect consciously to our wounds, we have a greater opportunity to heal.

Story: How the Soul Fracture Happened

In the beginning, there was only potential, and in the end, there is only potential. From the infinite possibilities of this potential, the Great Spirit of Amazing Love and Light manifested. The Great Spirit was conscious and aware, full of creativity and curiosity. Through the consciousness of the Love and the Light, the multiverse, with all its dimensions and realities, was actualized. The great Source energy ("God" or "the Divine") contains all Love, all knowledge, all wisdom, and all things imaginable (and unimaginable). The Love and the curiosity led the expansion of consciousness to produce a myriad of souls, all of which were one with the Divine and with one another. As the souls claimed their individual consciousness and realized their potential, the freedom to experience was established through the gift of free will. This free will became part of the souls' individuality, and the individual and collective perspective was born. But in that primordial moment, many souls experienced a tearing-away from the Divine. As they discovered their free will, the souls misinterpreted the alignment Source holds with Love, and the gifts of free will and individuality were experienced as a traumatic event.

The Divine did not intend that the souls should suffer from this separation. It was, however, the only way for the souls to experience and to grow, to advance and interact with the infinite potential, and to learn about themselves—and it was the only way for Source to stay in integrity with Love. The Divine's Love is so true that these little souls were free to play in the illimitable energies and frequencies; to experience different dimensions, timelines, and vibrational energies high and low; and to do great things in both the power of the light and in the lure of the dark.

Now it is time for all of us beautiful souls to heal. Can you see that the Love from Source is true? We can always turn to the Divine for the direction and assistance that is available to all souls—but at the same time we have the freedom to ignore it and to exercise our free will. It is in our nature both to be free and aligned with Divine guidance simultaneously.

As we choose to remember and align to our true nature, the Love from Source becomes more apparent. We realize that the confusion and pain we suffer might just be bigger than what we have experienced in our current lifetime. Indeed, the root of our pain and suffering transcends our personal childhood, our ancestral lines, our soul family, even our karma. The root of all suffering is found in that single traumatic moment when Source gave us our greatest gift in accordance with Love: The Divine endowed our individual souls with free will. In that elemental moment, our souls experienced a fracturing of our energy fields. It was our free will, our *freedom* to *experience* that led us (indeed, allowed us) to misunderstand the positive intent behind our disconnection from the Divine. But despite our misinterpretation of this sublime act of Loving separation, we still have the opportunity to heal our fractured souls and find our way back to the truth. We may yet come to know ourselves once again as undifferentiated parts of the Whole of Source and as Divine expressions of Love. Source Loves us, so we are free. Love has no attachments. Love has no agenda. Love is exquisite, pure potential. Love is acceptance, freedom, power, and light. Love is us.

Forgiveness of Soul Wound

Forgiveness of Soul Wound

In order to heal fully, we must forgive both ourselves and Source for the wound we carry. Forgiveness makes our energy soft. Forgiveness releases any emotional charge. Forgiveness is the return to Love.

Healing the Soular Wound

Healing the Soular Wound

Once we have connected to the soular wound, we are able to heal it. If you haven't worked with the Soular Wound Light Code, (See "Soular Wound" on page 22-23.) please consider engaging with those energies before working with this Light Code.

It is possible not only to heal the soular wound, in truth, it is already healed. In order to embrace this healing, we can connect with the soular wound and be quiet with the energies that arise. Give yourself the ultimate gift of self-Love. Listen—what do your wounds wish to share? Once you have acknowledged those wounds, you can connect with the energy of this Light Code and be a witness to your own wound, already healed.

Releasing the Energies Associated
with the Soular Wound

Releasing the Energies Associated with the Soular Wound

This Light Code works in tandem with Forgiveness of the Soular Wound Light Code (see page 28-29). This Code helps us to release the energies which might be entangled with the soular wound, including karmic energies and forgiveness.

Chapter 3

Connecting with the Heart

All About the Heart

The heart center or "heart chakra" is the fourth major chakra in the traditional seven-chakra energy system of the human body—it is the point at which the physical realm meets the spiritual realm. The energetic heart center has an infinite capacity to feel and express Love. Although our wounded self builds walls around our heart in order to protect us, our wounds can heal completely. It is through activating our heart center that we connect with our higher self, our soul, and Source energy.

The Physical Heart

From a physiological point of view, our heart beats in a dynamic rhythm, pumping oxygenated blood throughout our physical body. The heart's dynamic rhythm range (heart rate variability) is important to our overall health and wellbeing, and its reach is determined by how well we cope with life's stressors. For example, a person with a greater heart rate variability is better able to navigate life more easily and "go with the flow." Because of the range of their heart rate variability, they are able to recover from various stressors in a reasonable time frame. This allows the body to stop losing energy over whatever caused the stress and to repair and rejuvenate itself. In contrast, a person who has a limited heart rate variability might be less likely to "go with the flow" and therefore be less capable of recovering from stress. In this scenario, the person stays stressed for longer, and loses valuable energy. Energy loss is related to poor health, challenging relationships, and even lowered intelligence. Coping and managing stress becomes key to living a long and healthy life.

The physical heart and nervous system are inter-connected and both play an important role in stress management. Practicing simple exercises can bring the physical heart into better alignment with the nervous system, and can help us reduce stress and lead a healthier life overall. Researchers have found that the nervous system not only impacts the physical heart, but that there is an interplay between the nervous system and the electromagnetic field the heart produces. We can learn to self-regulate our physiological and emotional responses using simple exercises such as those taught by HeartMath®. I recommend a visit to HeartMath.com for more information.

The Energetic Heart

To have access to our heart is to have access to our soul. When we are able to shed the layers and blocks we have placed around our hearts, a door opens within us to reveal incredible, powerful aspects of ourselves. We are better able to process our reactions to what people say and do (or don't do), taking less offence and eventually learning that we should not take things personally. Opening our heart expands our ability to navigate life with greater ease and understanding. As we rediscover that our heart is our ultimate guide, we bring forward our authentic Love and can develop our intuition on new levels, paving the way for pure connection to the higher realms of existence.

When we are connected to our empowered heart (and not our wounded heart), our heart will lead us in the perfect direction. Living our optimum life is less about what we are doing day-to-day, it's more about being connected to our heart while we live our physical lives. The message: "I am on my path when I am in my heart" resonates here. So, stay true to your heart—stay true to your journey. Do things that make you feel happy, that inspire gratitude, and that bring you a sense of pride and accomplishment. Practice releasing and letting go, and then fill your energy body with Light. (See: Mental Exercise for Letting Go (see page 64) and Fill Your Body with Light (see page 84)).

Heart Connection

While you explore heart opening and healing on all levels, questions may arise for you:

- ☺ How do I activate my heart?
- ☺ How do I get in touch with this amazing part of myself? and
- ☺ How do I ask questions of my heart in a way that facilitates clear questions and answers?

Expansion of the Heart

Expansion of the Heart

Light Codes and Light Language transmissions that have been channeled energetically with pure, clean Love, speak directly not only with your heart but with your whole being. By meditating with the Codes and by holding a clear intention in your mind, you can connect deeply with your heart. (The Codes in this book and in *The Little Book of Light Codes* by Laara are ideal tools to help you open up your heart.)

Exercise to Feel Your Heart

1. Begin by slowing your breath. Close your eyes if it is comfortable for you to do so. Bring your attention to your feet. When you feel relaxed, continue to breathe slowly and focus your attention on your heart space. Try to feel your feet at the same time you feel your heart space. Feel the expansion of your heart space with every breath—and anchor this expansion down to your feet by bringing your awareness to both of these locations simultaneously.

2. Once you can feel your heart, you can ask questions and know the answers intuitively. The answers can come in a variety of ways: knowing, sensing/feeling, hearing, seeing, or smelling. Sometimes we must wait to receive the answers we are seeking. Remain patient. Allow the answers to come to you in divine timing.

Don't make it more complicated than this! It is truly this simple. Like everything, the more we practice, the more proficient we become. Remember, you are whole, complete, beautiful, and in need of nothing. You not only have all the answers, in the depths of your soul you *are*—and since the beginning of time *always have been*—all the answers.

Beauty Beholds the Soul

Beauty Beholds the Soul

We follow our heart into all things beautiful—as beauty calls forward our heart and our Love. In the ancient world, the Neoplatonist philosopher Plotinus stated that " … the soul that beholds beauty becomes beautiful." But rather than believing that the "soul beholds beauty," consider for a moment the converse: that beauty itself can behold the soul. What does this mean? When you express your true self—the self that abides within your soul—when you are comfortable with who you are and you resonate the Love That You Are from the inside out, you are beauty itself. You can gaze upon the Light of your soul as in a mirror, and reveal the pure Love that reflects your soul. Perhaps meditate upon this Light Code, and explore the frequencies emitted. How do they resonate within your being? There is no right or wrong. Simply *experience*. Allow beauty, in all its forms as a divine expression of Love, to wash over you. Take it in. Breathe it in. Be with whatever comes. When you are ready, release the experience.

Love and Trauma

As we move through our physical lifetime, the experiences we have can change the range of vibration we hold. We feel Love and our frequency expands. We encounter trauma and our resonance can collapse. This is why, when we are unhappy, we aren't in our Love (our optimal vibration) and we aren't "ourselves." Some of the trauma we encounter has minimal impact upon our being, although at the time, it can feel emotionally and physically intense. This type of trauma can impact our life, but may not be carried forward or passed into alternate lifetimes. If our being is unable to navigate a trauma masterfully, the effect of the trauma can reach the soul and compound the soular fracture. These wounds remain with us and contribute to ancestral energies, which are passed down generationally until they are healed.

Soul Groups and Trauma

The soul longs to experience—and ultimately to heal—all of the energetic fractures it has attained. As it does so, it contributes to the healing of the larger "soul family" and the healing of all souls—remember the primeval separation of the soul from Source? While our soul is separate, it is also part of a greater, dynamic, energetic whole, and healing can be shared among all souls.

Each soul is an energetic frequency unique unto itself. This vibration, while distinctive to each soul, is contained within the vibratory range of Love. As a soul, we interact with a large group of souls who share a similar resonance. Souls are classified into groups often referred to as Soul Bands, Soul Trees, and other terms which describe the categorization of souls who share a similar energetic resonance. This group can change as we experience life and develop karmic ties. For example, if we experience a catastrophic life event, it will be felt on the soul level. If this event is experienced with others, it can create an energetic connection which will create a new Soul Band. This group of souls can reincarnate together or assist one another in some way. The karma and trauma from an event of this magnitude will be imprinted on the soul level, and like all trauma, will be in need of forgiveness and release (healing). Until the trauma has been forgiven and released, the energetic mark upon the soul is similar to a physical wound making a mark upon our physical body. Even with the biggest traumas it's important to remember that all trauma is energy, and Love is the ultimate healer of all wounds (both physical and emotional). Each time we rise to and overcome a challenge, our soul grows and our vibration increases as the healing creates a deeper connection to the Love That We Are.

If we have created a new Soul Band connection due to a shared traumatic event, it's important to know that we will never "lose" our previous soul-band family. This is because outside of our third-dimensional reality there is no time and space, and ultimately, *no separation*. All existence is occurring *now*: Past, present, and future occur *in this moment* simultaneously. It is our interpretation and perception of this reality that leads us to the illusion of time and space. On the soul level, we are all one within a single point of existence.

Story: Soul Colors

We can think of the soul as a single drop of water in the ocean. The molecules that make up that individual droplet are connected to all the other molecules that make up all of the water droplets in the ocean. The ocean our soul swims in is the ocean of Divine Oneness and pure Love. And just like a fish that swims in a tropical ocean teeming with color and movement, our soul is alive with the unique soular frequency of Love. Together with all the other souls in our soul family, we create a vast energetic field vibrating in a rainbow of color.

While all colors are expressed by each individual soul, there will be more dominant colors for each soul depending upon their "position" within the greater whole. On the soul level, we are grouped by color, the same way colors are grouped within the spectrum of the rainbow. The colors originate from within the energy of Source. The occupation—or *placement*—within Source's energy in which each soul resides determines our dominant colors. The *location* remains infinite, unattached to a specific orientation because Source and soul reside in an existence beyond time and space. This "color organization" is the basis of Soul Bands, Soul Ties, Soul Trees, and other terms that describe the connection of souls in oneness.

Although the dominant colors will be the same for each soul within a soul family, every soul expresses all colors. For example, a "blue" soul family will have a blue hue overtone to their essence, but all colors still emanate from their field. All colors possible in existence will be represented within each soul, within the soul family, and by the collective soul, as well as by Source.

The Soul's Journey with Love and Dimensions

The Soul may choose to incarnate on a planet and experience what it would be like to play in a different dimension. The soul focuses its consciousness into a narrow band of frequency in order to manifest in the physical realm. The soul chooses when and where and into what physical expression it will incarnate. The higher the life form, the more potential there is to work with a wider array of energies. If it's choosing a human, animal, or plant experience, the soul chooses the family, species, or genus into which to incarnate. The more complex the life form, the fuller the range of potential for self-discovery and expression—but there is also more opportunity to get into trouble. Since Divine Love is unconditional and Source allows the soul to be free in accordance with Love, the soul is free to get into as much trouble as it likes. But there are Universal Laws governed by Love, and one of these Laws states that if a soul wishes to be destructive and act *out of accordance* with Love, then the soul must continue incarnating in a lower density experience. This is because although Love allows for all potential expression (including acting in discord with the principles of Love), Love will not allow Love to be unloving without consequence. When a soul acts out of alignment with Love, it is not loving, and it is not in harmony with truth. Truth is Love, Love is truth. This means that if a soul wishes to advance to a higher-frequency dimension, it must operate in accordance with Love and truth. The higher the frequency of a dimension or realm, the less obstructed Love becomes. As we climb the frequency ladder, becoming more and more in alignment with the truth of Love, eventually we connect to the infinite possibilities which reside beyond Love. In the end there is only potential, but before the infinite collapses, we are all expressions of Love.

Reconnecting to Eternal Joy

Reconnecting to Eternal Joy

Our soul is an expression of joy in the highest form, because Love is joy! With the experience of joy is the deep realization that there are no limitations. The only limitations are those we impose upon our self. When we subscribe to limiting thoughts and beliefs (anything other than "I am pure Love"), we entrap our mind, causing it to *believe that falsities are truth*. By reconnecting to our eternal joy, we transcend lower vibrational and dysfunctional energies (falsities), realigning with the Love That We Are.

Breathe deeply and tune into the lightness of eternal joy: a joy which resides at the core of your being.

Take It Easy

In order to feel joy at the soul level, we must focus our attention on the energies present within our life. While we contemplate some of the profound stories and energies offered by the Light Codes, we can take notice of what is simultaneously occurring in our lives *right now*. It's easy to be confused by outside influences and opinions, gossip, and other distractions that take us away from "this moment." We can even feel pressure that everything must happen all at once, or that things should look a certain way. It has been well established that time is not a fixed construct; as individuals, we all have our own perception and experience of time. In general, many of us human beings are feeling as though time is speeding up. This is, in part, due to the astrological transition of Ages we are currently experiencing. We are moving from the watery sign of Pisces into the airy sign of Aquarius, which transition takes hundreds of years to complete. Typically, air moves faster than water, and the consequence of this is expressed through our perception that time is amplified.

Humanity in general has made a fundamental error with this perceived increase in time—as many of us struggle to pack more "life" into each day. But the increase of time, in actuality, is a *compression* of time. Imagine if time was expressed as a fluffy loaf of sliced bread. As we move deeper into the Age of Aquarius, the single slices of bread are compressed and compacted, taking less space within the loaf, and thus altering how we experience the passage of time. We can use this phenomenon to our advantage:

This compression is best used to speed up our healing process! Instead of taking months, years, or lifetimes to heal, we can use the natural compression of time to heal ourselves faster. Rather than working against time (wishing we had more of it, for example), we could use it to our benefit. As noted earlier, we are in the Age of Purification—we need to purify the energies within and around us to bring us back into alignment with our Love and release the energies which no longer serve us in our Highest Good. Increased time is meant as an asset, not as a weight. Worrying about getting everything done perfectly detracts from the eternal beauty and joy held within the soul. Allow yourself the time and space to discover the role you occupy in this play called life, and feel the expansion and connection to your soul's joyful nature.

Joyful Expression of the Whole Soul

Joyful Expression of the Whole Soul

With levels of the soular wound healed and released, we can bring forward more healing by tuning into the joyful expression of the soul. This is more easily felt as we connect on a deeper level to our heart. All of the people, places, and things which bring forward your heart (your Love) align you perfectly with your highest consciousness, desire, and purpose.

Chapter 4

Letting Go

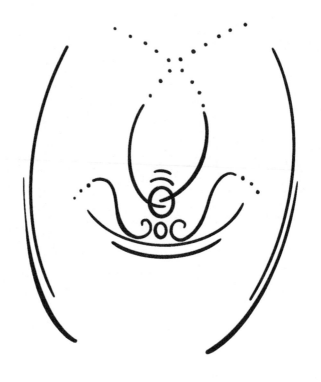

Trusting Our Love

Trusting Our Love

The act of letting go of attachments—of people or situations, thoughts or behaviors, or things that upset or limit us—is a skill that we must learn in order to stay in alignment with our heart. If we are attached to something, we aren't in harmony with the universe and we are resisting the natural flow of Love. One reason letting go is often challenging for us is that we fear the result. When we feel fear, we aren't in our Love. When we are connected to and experiencing life from our higher aspects—more connected to our Love—letting go is easy! It's our lower aspect of self, our ego, which has a tendency to form attachments because our ego expresses our wounds. As we heal our soular wounds, we are also healing our ego. Part of the healing process is consciously breaking habits and attachments which no longer serve us in our highest good. When we notice an attachment, we have an opportunity to release it, bless it, and ask for the highest outcome for all to reveal itself. In order to act in accordance with Love and remain in alignment, we need to trust our Love.

Mental Exercise for Letting Go

Imagine you are holding a pen up in the air. Now release the grip you have on the pen. This is how frustratingly simple letting go can be. How are we able to let go of upset this easily? By practicing. Practice letting go constantly. First, practice letting go of things that don't cause you upset, that aren't challenging to release from within your being. Do simple exercises to practice letting go, so that when a challenging situation arises, your physical, mental, and emotional bodies are well-versed in how to release.

Letting Go Meditation
Step 1:
Adopt a comfortable position, sitting, standing, or lying down. Your eyes may be open or closed. Inhale deeply. While you hold your breath, tighten all of the muscles in your body and hold for three to five seconds. Relax and exhale out of your mouth. Feel the tension melting out of your body. The next time you try this, when you exhale out of your mouth and relax, imagine and feel the tension going down into the earth.

Step 2:
Take a couple of deep breaths. This time, try to relax your entire body on the inhale. As you exhale out of your mouth, relax and melt into the earth. Allow any tension to dissolve into the ground with every exhale: Thoughts, muscle tightness, excess energy, lack of energy—let it all go.

Step 3:
Reframe. Instead of thinking you need to "let go" of something, simply allow the thought or upset to melt, release, or sink into the earth as you exhale through your mouth.

Release All Expectations

Release All Expectations

Similar to attachments, *expectations* and *wanting* serve only as obstacles in the natural flow of the universal ocean. They create a spark of energy which disrupts the ease of flow. Imagine the flow of energy being the ripple a raindrop creates when it falls into a still pond. The act of wanting creates a disruption in the ripple. Be aware— what do you expect? What do you want? Do your desires serve the current situation? Do they support the energetic dynamics of the situation? Are these energies in the best-ever alignments? Or do your desires disturb the current flow?

In any given case it can behoove us to be more aware of our expectations and of the reactions in response to our wants and desires, both from the universe and from the people around us. Sometimes it's good to want, but sometimes the act of wanting only disrupts a good thing. For example: Perhaps we have a strong desire to be in a relationship and we work hard to make a relationship happen. But before entering into a relationship, we might be better off single as we continue to heal and align with the Love within us. This way, when we do find a partner, we aren't bringing in unnecessary expectations, beliefs, and wounds that could have a negative effect on the partnership. If we are patient and remain open to having an amazing relationship while continuing to connect to the Love That We Are, we will be in flow with the universe and attract an amazing alignment with a partner. Expectations, big or small, are a creation of the ego.

Story: The Story of the Ego

In order for the soul to learn about itself and to heal, grow, and expand, the soul chooses to experience a life incarnated in the third dimension. The realm in which the soul resides is a very high frequency, so high that a physical body exposed to such a frequency would cease to exist. In order for the soul to experience a physical life, it needs to project parts of itself into a lower density. The soul does this in stages, from the soul level down to the higher self, to the heart, and finally to the lower self (ego). Each progressive stage is denser and "further away" from the true, high vibratory energy of the soul (the Love That We Are). The soul projects down to the lower self the wounds it wishes to learn about and heal, and the energies of these wounds become stronger as their density increases.

The ego is our identity with physical reality. It plays an integral role in the soul's ability to learn, play, and explore in the physical realm and it is through the ego that the soul connects to the physicality of what it wants to learn about. In the physical world our ego is given a name (such as "Jackie" or "Peter"), and depending on what our soul came to experience, our ego is given free will to play with personalities, likes, and wants. Our ego might have a variety of desires—for example, it might like to wear flamboyant clothes, listen to classical music, or express itself through modern dance. How well we are able to listen to our hearts will determine if these expressions are in alignment with our Love (soul).

The ego's job is to facilitate our physical experience: to navigate our basic survival needs (food, shelter, safety, procreation), to express our personality (traits, habits, likes, dislikes, wants, and desires), and to be a servant to the soul's reason (or mission) for incarnating. As human beings, we've been taught that the ego is also responsible for our self-awareness, health, self-esteem, and so on. It is true that the ego is helpful in navigating circumstances that may be questionable or dangerous to our physical, mental, and emotional bodies, but the ego should *only* act at the direction of the higher aspects of ourselves. This concept has been misunderstood and that has caused us to place blocks around our hearts. The heart (which communicates with the higher self and the soul) should direct the ego, not the other way around.

In our early years, family dynamics and culture can suppress the ways in which our heart directs our ego. In an effort to conform to societal pressures and in search of acceptance, the ego learns to usurp the heart's direction. However, our lower self (the ego which commands our thinking-brain) *thinks* it needs to do *a lot* more work than what it was designed to do—it believes it needs to protect us! This is NOT its design. Through culture, schooling, family, friends, ancestral energies, traumas, belief systems, and the soular wound, the ego learns to believe that it alone can save us. So, with the grace of a bull in a china shop, the ego takes command of our third dimensional life experience. Once the ego has taken command, it is operating outside its designed function and it has lost valuable contact with higher vibrational guidance and direction. The ego has no choice but to engage with lower vibrational energies (with which it has closer resonance), and in doing so, it creates an unstable foundation for health, happiness, and abundance. We become more open to outside influences because our inner authority is compromised.

We continue to give away our inner authority as we look for acceptance, direction, and Love from outside of ourselves. Now others can hurt us. Fear begins to brew and we cling to anything and everything that brings us comfort. The lower self (which by this time is not listening to the direction of the heart for fear of being hurt), build walls around the heart—because our heart takes in emotion deeply. If we don't have the tools to process emotion properly, it can be challenging for the heart to transmute the energy. These walls cut us off from our higher self and soul. We are now separated from our true nature and from Source energy; we are weak and vulnerable. The result? Various levels of dysfunction: poor health, stress, anxiety, bad relationships, poor communication, and even decreased intelligence.

We must learn how to transcend the dysfunction of our ego while still honoring and embracing being an incarnated human being with an ego. When the ego is in its appropriate place (as a servant to our higher aspects), we can more easily create a reality in alignment with the Love That We Are.

Meditation

Sit quietly. Breathe deeply. The ego can relax and let go of all concern. All control. All restrictions. The ego has a much easier job to do than what it has taken on. The ego can relax. There is nothing for it to do but follow the simple, loving guidance and direction from the higher self in accordance with (my) Love.

Affirmation

Repeat:

"My ego doesn't need any responsibility other than to follow my heart's direction. It will naturally and easily take care of my basic needs."

Transitioning with Ease

Transitioning with Ease

Be like a butterfly. Navigate the energies within and around you with ease and softness. Flutter about in search of nectar, move gracefully away from places or situations that no longer align with your truth. Live in the moment. Witness. Observe. Be Love. Always ask yourself, "What would Love do?" My name is Love, dear reader. What is yours?

Repeat:

"My name is Love."

"I choose to live my life in accordance with Love."

What Is Love?

You can live a loving life like a butterfly, soft and sweet, agile and discerning. You can love all those who cross your path, knowing they are on their own path. But Love is being strong. Love is having boundaries. Love is living in authenticity and truth. Love is the energy with which consciousness was born, whole and complete. Love is abundant and full, natural and infinite. Love lacks nothing, is inclusive of all, and functions from the highest integrity.

Repeat:

"I am safe, for I am Love. Love is honoring. Love is respect. Love is acceptance. Love is knowing thyself. Love is loving thyself. Love is letting go of all attachments. I am light. Nothing weighs me down, like a butterfly. Love, be like a Butterfly."

Higher Self Energy Stream

Higher Self Energy Stream

This symbol can assist us in connecting with the energies of the ego so we can show ourselves gently that our ego has taken on roles that don't belong to it. These roles belong to other parts of our being, namely our heart, higher self, and soul. We can relieve our ego of unnecessary stresses and stop feeling as though we are carrying the weight of the world on our shoulders.

Since our thinking brain is directly connected to our ego (the ego actually "runs" the thinking brain), it can be helpful to use mind-relaxing tools in order to soothe our ever-active ego. When our ego (thinking brain) is relaxed, we have a better opportunity to connect with our heart and receive direction from the higher aspects of ourselves. This way, we can tune into better decisions, directions, and alignments, as well as an increased sense of wellbeing.

Thinking too much or being in a state of incoherence can block the transmissions of the heart. When we are "in our head," we are restricting a channel of awareness to receive the heart's messages.

Meditation: Relax the Mind

Sit quietly with this message, perhaps engaging with the Letting Go meditation or Exercise to Feel Your Heart. Relax. Breathe deeply and slowly. Let your mind soften, let your heart speak. You don't need to have everything figured out in one day. It may feel like you're running to catch up or keep up, but in reality, all you need to do is relax your mind.

Nothing Is Personal

Nothing Is Personal

It is common for us to take other people's words, actions, inactions, or the situations that occur in their lives personally. We fail to realize that what other people do (or don't do) is purely a reflection of their own inner wound, process, and journey. When we take things personally, we are reacting in a conditioned manner—which can lead only to pain and suffering. Taking things personally fills us with confusion and leads to disappointment. The wounding that rises from unrealized expectations adds to our sense of separation and lack, impelling us to seek solutions to soothe our hurt feelings and relieve our suffering. Returning again and again to these solutions is called "addiction."

Addiction

We are rarely upset for the reason we think. The truth is, when we are hurt or offended by someone's actions or because something has happened to upset us, often it will serve us best to set the situation aside and look instead at the bigger picture: the soular wound. The soular wound can create a variety of emotional energies which we experience as humans, such as feeling unloved, unwanted, unworthy, not good enough, abandoned, or neglected (to name a few). All of these emotions can be distilled down to a single feeling and energy: lack. We call it "lack" because we are lacking our Love. When we are full of our Love (which happens as we heal the soular wound), we don't resonate with any of the aforementioned examples. This sense of lack creates the feeling of a void deep within, and we feel subconsciously driven to fill this void. For most of us, since our ego is currently in charge, we search for answers outside of ourselves and can get caught trying to fill our void with destructive and repetitive behavior.

How do you think you would feel if you healed your soular wound? Would you be able to cease looking for ways to fill the void within you?

Addiction: repeating a behavior which is
trying to fill a void.

Void: a perceived lack of Love and Self.

Plasma Crystal Healing

Plasma Crystal Healing

This Light Code is offering to show us the addictive tendencies we find ourselves caught in from time to time. It can be difficult for us to see addiction clearly within ourselves and acknowledge it. So, the energies associated with this Code are soothing. It reminds us of our infinite capacity, while offering to help us balance our energy and restore our ability to receive Love. It offers a clearing of dysfunctional energies and lack of Love, alongside offering new energies to uplift and inspire. This Light Code can be used in conjunction with the exercise noted below—the conscious act of filling your physical body with Light.

Fill Your Body with Light

When you fill your body with Light, in essence, you are raising your vibration. It is important to fill your body with Light often—you can do it easily and organically! Participate in activities that bring you happiness and joy, activities in alignment with your heart. You can fill your body with Light consciously with various practices. Here are some ideas:

- Breath Work
- Yoga
- Tai Chi
- Qi Gong
- Meditation
- Dance
- Eating whole foods
- Drinking fresh spring water
- Playing singing bowls
- Diffusing essential oils.

The key point in any of these vibration-raising activities is to engage fully, with conscious awareness. This means that you focus on your purpose: in this case, becoming present, grounding yourself, and filling your body with Light.

Many meditation practices and multidimensional experiences are helpful in filling the body with Light, such as Fractalline Healing™ (check out fractallinehealing.com). The Grounding Practice mentioned in Chapter 1 of this book is also an appropriate tool for raising your vibration. I highly recommend it.

Chapter 5

Love and Relationship

Manifest Your Love

Within all of our relationships (and even outside of them), it is important always to be mindful, moment to moment, of striving for a coherent connection between our heart and mind. Even as we examine the relationships we share with others, we must never forget the importance of the relationship we have with ourselves. For as our coherence level increases, so does our connection with our heart, and so does the Love That We Are. This helps us to facilitate healthier relationships with those with whom we are divinely aligned. From a coherent heart space, we can radiate our Love outward, standing in stillness within our being, opening ourselves consciously and fully to all of the relationships that are in our highest alignment. Free of attachments, free of intense desires, and free of all of the limiting creations of our ego mind, we can allow others to experience the Love we feel toward them, while knowing in the deepest part of ourselves that we are already that Love. *You are that Love.* When we own this fact, it helps others whom we love to find this Love within themselves. Some people may not understand what is happening, but they will feel our Love nonetheless.

So, how can we hold this Loving space? By doing what we do, but doing it even more! Stay on top of your personal responsibilities. Do your self-care. Continue practicing coherence (or if you haven't taken up a practice already, look into those offered by HeartMath®). Remember, it's your choice to bring forward the joy and the Love That You Are. Make a conscious choice—set a powerful intention—to anchor your authentic, loving being into this physical dimension, as the ultimate divine expression of your Love.

Remember, when you are using the Light Codes to manifest your Love into reality (whether in the form of a relationship or something else), tune into as many senses as possible—see, hear, smell, and taste—and feel the power of your Love pouring forth into reality. Feel its healing energy. The section below contains affirmations for and information about the healing frequencies emitted by specific Light Codes. Combining the affirmations with the frequencies is powerful, so remember: Work with language that resonates with you. Change the language as needed, and create your own affirmations where necessary. Speak the affirmations aloud while meditating upon the Light Code.

The Divine Feminine and the Divine Masculine

We all have a balance of feminine and masculine energies within us. Feminine energy is soft, nurturing, and graceful, while masculine is powerful, strong, and courageous.

The Divine Feminine

The Divine Feminine

The Divine Feminine energies represent creativity, empathy, and vulnerability. Within the feminine energies, we are receptive and open. This Light Code emanates all of the Divine Feminine qualities, helping us to connect with these sacred aspects of our self and bring them into optimal alignment.

The Divine Masculine

The Divine Masculine

Just as we can bring more consciousness and awareness to our Divine Feminine, we can do the same with our Divine Masculine energies. The masculine is an action-based aspect, as opposed to the feminine which is more receptive. With the Divine Masculine's emotional balance, confidence, and willpower, we can act upon the intuition and compassion gathered by the Divine Feminine. Meditate upon this Light Code to assist you in bringing balance to the masculine energies within your being.

New Relationship Paradigm – Balancing the Masculine and Feminine

As our society moves away from the masculine-dominant model that has governed for millennia, we are entering a new era in which relationships (especially those of a romantic nature) are becoming ever more conscious, balanced, and collaborative. In the new relationship paradigm, mutually beneficial equality and harmony across all fronts is paramount.

For example, in a romantic relationship, each person represents an entity of energy (with wants, needs, and desires), while the relationship itself also constitutes an entity (with wants, needs, and desires). In this case, three entities create the relationship. It is common, in dysfunctional relationships, for one, two, or all three entities to be compromised in some way, usually with one entity taking on a dominating role. They are not honored, equal, or in balance and harmony with one another, as a hierarchy is established. This hierarchy may not be conscious. It may be present due to traumas and wounds, as well as the greater cultural or societal energies each person's soul has chosen to engage with. In this arrangement, it is common for one or both partners to become energetically depleted, as the relationship isn't supportive of vibrant, healthy energy. One or both partners can become drained of energy or susceptible to illness or depression, and ultimately can be derailed from their soul mission.

In the new paradigm, there is no hierarchy as the people who are in the relationship together—and the relationship energy itself—are all on the same plane. This equality provides stability, health, vitality, and support for all entities that form the relationship. As many aspects as possible are held in balance, supporting the energy of the relationship (such as those in the relationship having a similar lifestyle or soul mission). In this new paradigm, the energy of the relationship is fulfilling, nurturing, and mutually beneficial. The relationship energies feed the individuals and the individuals feed the relationship, in a continuous cycle of Love.

Relationship Guide

Here are some practices you and your partner can do to deepen your relationship and bring about more balance between the entities in the relationship. This guide can be used for any relationship, it is not limited to those of a romantic nature.

- Check in with your heart and higher self often.
- Be the Love That You Are.
- Make changes as necessary to stay in alignment and accordance with Love.
- Take time for yourself every day, and share your needs / wants / desires as necessary with your partner(s).
- Share openly with your partner(s), while holding no fear. Communicate what's going on for you.
- Be receptive.
- Be inclusive but remain unattached. You are your own person.
- Be respectful and non-judgmental.
- Practice coherence-building exercises together (such as those from HeartMath®).

Healthy Relationship

Healthy Relationship

Everything in life can be viewed on the energetic plane, including relationships. There are energetic dynamics in constant motion within every relationship. Some are pleasant, some are challenging, but hopefully we will navigate them all to the best of our abilities. As noted earlier, in order for a relationship to remain healthy, functional, and mutually beneficial, each person and the relationship itself must be supported equally. When we are in a healthy relationship (romantic or otherwise), the energies of the relationship feed individuals and the relationship to enhance each party's state of wellbeing. A healthy dynamic will rarely (or minimally) detract or deplete the mental, emotional, physical, and spiritual energies from each person. The relationship will support growth and rejuvenation for those involved.

Releasing Relationships

Releasing Relationships

As we journey through our lifetime, we make connections and develop relationships with many people, animals, places, objects, habits/behaviors, and activities. Anything that we can form an attachment to or be in a relationship with (which is just about everything), will develop an energetic connection. When we are complete with a relationship (in whatever form it takes), the connection (or bond) we have developed needs to be honored and released appropriately. Whether we feel grateful for the relationship or not, every connection should be held in respect, as there is almost always a higher intent and lesson to be learned for those involved. The energies need to be cleared from within and around our being, in order to move on fully and completely, with no confusion about the past and the dynamics we experienced. It's best to find a way to feel some gratitude for what we have experienced, knowing there was some part of us that needed to connect with the energies which "played out." We will therefore find it necessary to release dysfunctional and functional relationships, as well as the energies of completed relationships. It can be helpful to set clear intentions to release relationship energies, while remaining as calm and as heart-centered as possible.

You may choose to include the Affirmations below as you set your intentions.

Affirmations

- 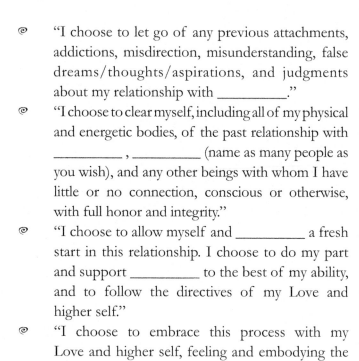 "I choose to let go of any previous attachments, addictions, misdirection, misunderstanding, false dreams/thoughts/aspirations, and judgments about my relationship with _____."

- "I choose to clear myself, including all of my physical and energetic bodies, of the past relationship with _____ , _____ (name as many people as you wish), and any other beings with whom I have little or no connection, conscious or otherwise, with full honor and integrity."

- "I choose to allow myself and _____ a fresh start in this relationship. I choose to do my part and support _____ to the best of my ability, and to follow the directives of my Love and higher self."

- "I choose to embrace this process with my Love and higher self, feeling and embodying the lightness, newness, and joy of this process."

- "I ask for continued clarity, grace, and guidance in my pursuit of Self-Love and Self-acceptance, as I fulfill my personal mission in this life."

- "I choose to release all of my personal agendas and my participation in all other persons' agendas, known and unknown, in my highest good and the highest good for all."

 "I choose for all of these declarations to be fulfilled and carried out in accordance with the Love That I Am, for my higher self, in my highest good, and for the highest good of all."

Complete your affirmation(s) with:
"So it is."

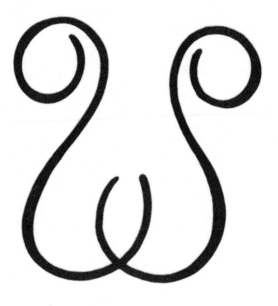

Twin Flames

Twin Flames

For many of us, the attraction of a "Twin Flame"(or a "Twin Soul" as they are also known), is irresistible. But while their pull is magnetic, engaging in a relationship with a Twin Flame is for many people a spiritual trap—Twin Flame energy can be a low vibrational energy that usually draws us into pain and suffering.

So, what are Twin Flames? Prior to incarnating on the physical plane, our soul has the ability to "split" into an infinite number of "personalities" and "expressions" in order to learn and come to know itself as part of the great interconnected consciousness of oneness. Your soul may live multiple incarnations on this 3D-earth plane ("Gaia") simultaneously, in linear existence. But, like a hologram that splits into pieces, each "part" is always "whole." Contrary to some popular theories, we *do not need* to be physically entangled with our other soul parts (our Twin Soul(s)) in order to become whole. In fact, to search for (or even engage with) another physical-manifestation of our soul in this lifetime can perpetuate pain and suffering. Why? Because our Twin Flame comes into this physical world to heal a different aspect of our shared soul—so a reunion in the physical world does not bring the love or healing we are seeking. Instead, it can impede both our healing and our Twin's healing. Ultimately, this dynamic can generate within both of us a yearning to return to the wholeness whence we came. Rarely can we live our best lives in union with our Twin Flame in the world. This is why, when we meet our "Twin," we seem to come together and fall apart—repeatedly. Even though each of us longs to return to the wholeness we once were, we know that we are meant to remain apart. So, instead of longing for that "one love," become open to ALL Love. This is where you will find your greatest levels of comfort, fulfillment, peace, and happiness in this lifetime. After all, these energies can never be found by looking outside yourself. So many of us form attachments which are by definition dysfunctional. Be open to Love: your Love, the Love of people, plants, animals, rocks, and everything in existence. It is in these things that you will form and enjoy your most fulfilling harmonic, easy relationships.

The Light Code offered for this topic is to assist in bringing greater levels of understanding, function, and balance to the Twin Flame energy.

Affirmations

- "I am a sublime eternal child who knows how to look after myself and connect to God: Source energy. Through the Love which runs through me always, this child knows how to navigate the 3D world, and all of the worlds, dimensions, and realms in all of space time."
- "I am curious, innocent, and open to the wonders of the universe."
- "I choose to be fully present in relationship with myself and others."
- "I choose to release all fear of hurt or rejection, knowing that Love will direct and be my guide to happiness and joy."
- "It is my goal and mission to learn how to play like the eternal child."
- "It is my goal and mission to do my Lightwork for myself and for the collective."
- "It is my goal and mission to remember and to be the Love That I Am."
- "How I do this doesn't matter, but I must remember to stay focused and free of entanglements and traps. Small breaks are okay. Working with others is okay. Asking for help is okay. Playing and working with energies often is the key. This is my purpose as a Lightworker, and the universe will provide abundantly so that all my needs are supported fully and completely."
- "I choose to release all fears around relationships and choose to know, deep within my being,

that every outcome shall be in accordance with my Love."

- "I choose to observe energy and not take on any energies which are not for me in my highest good."

- "I choose to release fully and completely any non-essential entanglements and attachments in my life, in accordance with the Love That I Am."

Balanced Divine
Masculine and Feminine

Balanced Divine Masculine and Feminine

Through the emotional embrace of intuition, the Divine Feminine opens to receive all the wisdom and knowledge the universe has to offer. She shares, heart open, with the Divine Masculine, who receives with his Love all that she gives. He uses his power, strength, and command to step forward into the realm of unlimited possibilities, and to co-create with the Divine Feminine in a harmonious union of balanced, sacred energies.

Embrace and Celebrate Sexuality

Embrace and Celebrate Sexuality

Through the balance of giving and receiving, the Divine Masculine and the Divine Feminine bring forth their highly-charged energies and enter a state of sacred creative union. The energetically-charged expression of Love between them enhances each Divine entity. This Light Code is calling forward the beautiful, powerful energies of our manifestation, expressed by the balanced masculine and feminine. In the interplay and interchange of sublime energy, they are in complete harmony. Celebrate both aspects as one, and embrace the infinite potential of this sacred alliance.

Chapter 6

Becoming Masterful

Attractor Field: Positive Energy Space

Attractor Field: Positive Energy Space

Affirm: "I have chosen to upgrade to a Positive Energy Space, as I have released all Negative Energy Space within me and all around me."

Like Attracts Like

One of the Universal Laws is that "Like Attracts Like." What does this mean? Our energetic body is comprised of negatively-charged ions. The stronger the charge and the more "full" we are energetically, the more we will attract. If we are living our lives in a negative headspace, that is, if we are thinking thoughts such as "I'm no good" or "nobody can love me," we will attract negativity. If we live our lives through a positive mindset, such as "I feel good" or "I am grateful," we will attract positivity. This is the fundamental reasoning behind the Law of Attraction: Like Attracts Like. In order to attract positivity, we need to become an attractor field for positivity! The more we increase the density of our energy field with positive energy, the more powerful we become—because our energetic charge is stronger. We need to become increasingly more aware of what we desire and what we choose to attract because as we increase our energetic density, our thoughts become more powerful.

Affirmations

- "I choose to release attachments."
- "I choose to free myself on all levels from that which no longer serves me."
- "I am ready, willing, and able to release all that no longer serves me in my highest good."
- "I choose to release all that keeps me from being, expressing, and embodying fully and completely the Love That I Am."
- "I choose to release all emotion which prevents me from truth."
- "I choose to release all programs and beliefs which keep me from truth."
- "I choose to transmute and release all negative energy space within me and around me."
- "I choose to integrate my authentic self more fully and completely."
- "I live my life from the wisdom of my heart and soul mind."
- "I choose to let go and release illusions and confusion."
- "I choose to trust my brothers and sisters who are one with me."
- "I choose to bring forth my infinite Love."
- "I choose to be okay."

- "I choose to heal my liver."
- "I choose to heal my entire digestive system."
- "I choose to release all sickness as it is an illusion."
- "I choose to release mis-identity of the brain and body."

Optimal Human Body Function

Optimal Human Body Function

Pain and suffering are an intense experiential illusion, which is itself a polarity to our true nature as the Love That We Are. When we heal the soular fracture, the illusions we experience lessen in strength, and we return to our nature as a divine, sublime being of Love.

The illusions we believe can manifest as physical, mental, and emotional dis-ease. How is it fair to think that our body can function in perfection (which it is designed for and has the intelligence to do), when we have a fragmented sense of self at the core of our being? We blame our bodies for "having a mind of their own." We blame our parents for passing down faulty genes. We blame the circumstances of our childhood, our education, our culture, and our society for all the things we experience as being "wrong" with us. In reality, there is nothing wrong with us except that we hold a false sense of self. In truth, we have the authority, power, and potential to shift our illusionary, third-dimensional reality in a nanosecond. So, why can't we do it? Why can't we simply take command of the tiniest energetic particles that generate our physical body and physical experience? Answer: Because we don't have power and command over the energy we manifest. It takes a lot of energy to manifest in the physical world … energy most of us don't currently have easy access to. This is why we experience dysfunction in the form of dis-ease or the inability to create our dreams. The energy we lack, in part, is connected to the power we have given up throughout the life experiences that taught us we weren't capable. Many of us have been convinced through our upbringing that we simply can't do what our imaginations tell us we can! We haven't lived a life that has supported our greatness, as we were told continuously to seek outside ourselves for Love, acceptance, and answers. If we can take command of our energy, we can make miracles happen.

We see evidence of miracles every day—like the transitions in and out of our physical body in the form of birth and death. We see healing miracles that defy all medical science. We see supernatural events, like a forest fire that is burning out of control stopping at a property line, sparing one house out of many from destruction. Such events happen, to our utter amazement. (Amazement holds a certain kind of magic, but it shows us where we are limited by our beliefs. When we are amazed, we are overwhelmed with wonder—our belief has been challenged.)

With every act of awareness and consciousness, we have a direct opportunity to shift energies from a state of dysfunction to a state of optimal functionality. This applies to our physical body as well as to our energetic bodies. Below, we offer affirmations to support healthy body function, together with information about the healing frequencies emitted by each Light Code. As always, affirmations used in tandem with Light Codes can be a powerful combination, but remember: It is important to work with language that resonates with you. So, change the language as needed, or create your own affirmations as necessary. Speak each affirmation aloud while meditating upon the related Light Code. To increase the potential shifts of your reality, tune into as many senses as possible.

Affirmations

- "My body effortlessly cleanses and purifies."
- "My body finds it easy to release toxins and energies which are in my highest good to release."
- "My body performs natural functions effortlessly."
- "My body feels confident in performing all natural functions with ease."
- "My body is strong and capable."

As we take back our power and increase the positive energy within and around our being, we may need to take time and space for ourselves and re-evaluate how much (and what) we are responsible for within our lives. It can be helpful to write a list of all that you are responsible for, and check in with your heart and intuition as to whether or not it is in your highest good to continue with certain commitments. Taking responsibility for our own energy, commitments, likes, and dislikes helps us to come to know ourselves more deeply. We become more conscious of our Love and of the best alignment for our soul's journey.

Affirmation
Breathe deeply and ground yourself as you read aloud:

> "I am seeing and feeling the importance of going with the flow. I see and feel why it isn't best to make too many arrangements. I see the importance of being alone with myself. I honor the importance of having the time and space to check inward, to be with myself, and I know that working on the relationship with myself is the most important thing. Everything else in my life will fall into place in Divine Loving flow. I feel excited about getting to know myself more deeply."

Soul Wisdom, Integrated Human-Self

Soul Wisdom, Integrated Human-Self

As we slow ourselves down and become more present in the *now*, we make room to feel our higher self's wisdom consciously. To continue our growing self-mastery and healing, we connect and integrate the amazing wisdom, direction, and guidance from our higher aspects.

Light Codes can be helpful in assisting us to connect with this wisdom and higher aspects of ourselves, and to make a connection with the Light Codes we hold within our being. We are all made of Light Codes, since Light Codes are simply a Divine expression of information and energy. We as human beings are ready to carry *more* Light Codes within our physical body structures, which can help us to assimilate wisdom and information from our consciousness in higher planes. As the physical body is a vessel to condense, manage, and express energies in the third dimension, we need to include the physical body when we do our healings. A lot of energy is stored within our tissues, our organs, glands, muscle, fascia, tendons, and other parts of our physical body. The more we are able to work consciously with all of our bodies—mental, emotional, physical, and spiritual—the better we are able to heal.

In order to carry more Light Codes within our physical body, there needs to be an expansion on the physical cellular level (an upgrade) to take in the *new* information the Light Codes hold. This means of upgrade is circular: Light Codes bring expansion within the human body, and the more expanded we become, the more Light Codes we are able to hold. Light Codes are the easiest and most direct form of upgrade at this time.

A Message from Source

You have done nothing wrong, my child. You are literally perfect in every way. It's time for you to know this, deep within. There is no good or bad, right or wrong. There is only Love. Love has been confused, which is why you experience the polarities of Light and Dark and everything they represent in their extremes. But once you see Love as it truly is, there is no longer polarity. Nothing exists but Love. The physical realm, your current partial experience with consciousness (because there is much more to you than you are consciously aware of), is a playground of Love. Everything you can touch, feel, sense, see, smell, taste, experience, grow with, learn from … all this is Love. There is softness and sweetness and Light within all these experiences and expressions. All interactions. Love is everyone and everything. There is no sin.

You have done nothing wrong. A sinful act is simply an act lacking Love. The feedback you receive from these actions help you, through Love, to find direction, to find your way back to Love. Sin as you know it has not been used or thought of in the way Love intended.

You have done nothing wrong. You are experiencing! You are growing, learning, tasting life! You are doing exactly as you are meant to do. Keep doing it. Now, with greater clarity and understanding, you can attempt to see how Love is everything around you, all of the time. Forgiveness is Love, Love is forgiveness.

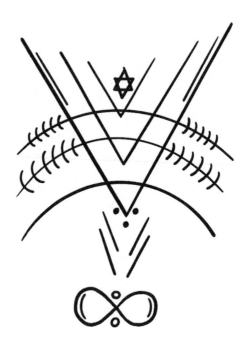

Integration of the Soular Wound

Integration of the Soular Wound

Integration and assimilation need to occur on all levels of our being. This symbol helps us to connect with healings on all levels, including the soul, higher self, and lower self. We bring the healing energies into our physical body, including into our mental and emotional bodies.

Free of the Soular Wound

Free of the Soular Wound

Once we have witnessed the wound, forgiven the wound, healed the wound, and released any associated energies of the wound, we can bring into our conscious awareness the reality of being free of the soular wound.

Chapter 7

Soul Connection

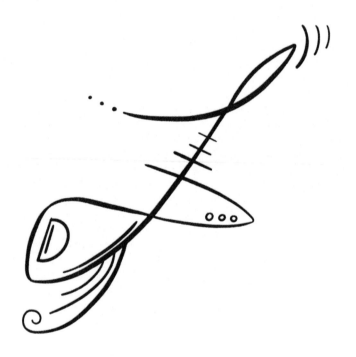

Soular Upgrades

Soular Upgrades

J ust as the human body receives upgrades that benefit our health, wellness, and connection to the Divine, the soul receives upgrades too. The soul is constantly perfecting itself and seeking to grow, expand, and know itself more deeply. Part of the fun of growth and expansion is receiving upgrades! Upgrades come from the infinite realm of possibilities, they come in many forms, and are conscious actualizations of multiple potential outcomes.

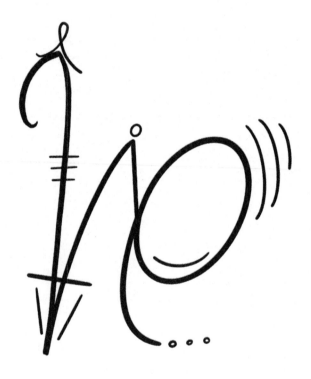

Soular Downloads

Soular Downloads

The soul can choose to share its wisdom and knowledge with the lower, physical aspect of itself by sending energetic information in the form of a "download." The physical body receives the information consciously or unconsciously, and may benefit by experiencing miracles and synchronicities, awakened gifts, and expanded talents.

Realignment of Personal Power

Realignment of Personal Power

When we are aligned and in balance with our center, our personal power is activated and strong. Our center is a column of Light, located in the middle of our physical body. It flows simultaneously upward and downward. When we are in our center, we know our Love, our wholeness, and our resilience. Our center is the authentic nature of our power, and when we are engaged with it, we are in flow with the rhythms of the universe.

A simple upsetting life event can be enough to push this column of Light off its centerline. For example, perhaps we take it personally when someone scowls at us for no apparent reason, and we feel some level of emotional upset. The energetic result of this interaction is that our column of Light slides off-center. The larger the event, assault, or trauma, the greater the potential "hit" to our column of Light. When our column of Light is affected, we are shown our wounds. What have we reacted to? Where within our being are we lacking Love?

Our column of Light can be pushed forward or backward, left or right, in response to a traumatic experience. This results in both an immediate loss of energy and a continuing loss of energy as the authentic power is not in perfect alignment in the center of the body. If the loss of energy is great enough for a long period of time, we may experience minor aches and pains, and even life-threatening conditions. This loss of energy also increases our chance of being a vibrational match to lower energies (such as viruses, bacteria, or fungi—all of which can potentially make our lives unpleasant).

This loss or imbalance of energy creates space in which illness can occur and addictive tendencies can take hold. We all have addictive tendencies. As mentioned earlier, they are a response to lack—a lack of energy, and ultimately, a lack of Love—all of which occur when we are off-center. In order to minimize the physical, mental, emotional, and spiritual effects of any cause-and-effect scenario, it's best to connect with our center (our authentic power) and work to bring it back into rightful alignment.

Most people are misaligned in this way and need to spend a bit of time working to bring their authentic power center back into balance. It can be helpful to use an affirmation such as "I choose to be in my authentic center of power" while at the same time adopting a lifestyle that is supportive of optimal alignment on all levels of your being. (Working with energy healing practitioners or holistic doctors—as well as practicing *Fractalline Healing* by Laara, a powerful healing modality—can also help you align your inner energy.)

Soul Connection Communication

Soul Connection Communication

Two of my Master teachers, Master Ling and Jeshua, teach us that we are never alone, for we are connected to the higher aspects of ourselves which watch over us always:

Dear One,

Please understand that one of our deepest desires is to know that we are not alone. We have a longing for connection at a fundamental level, and we seek this connection everywhere we can. This longing remains in our nature until our soular wound is healed.

In the meantime, our lives can be improved and enhanced by connecting to our soul; our ultimate Divine, sublime inner authority and power. Once we have established a connection with this Light channel, our world opens up in remarkable ways. We are able to tune into a broader range of frequencies, and thereby connect not only with the higher aspects of our self (such as our higher self and our soul), but also with the spirit realm.

Once we are able to shift and maintain a high enough baseline frequency, we will rarely feel alone. The higher our vibration or frequency is, the more we become a closer energetic match to higher frequency beings and energies, and the more easily we can connect with them.

—*Master Ling and Jeshua*

Use this Light Code to assist you in clearing the channels associated with communication on higher planes of existence. Although this Light Code is for soul communication, it will assist with all levels of communication because it helps to align us more clearly with the higher vibratory frequencies held within our soul.

Chapter 8

Activation

Galactic Consciousness

Galactic Consciousness

Galactic Consciousness refers to our conscious connection to galaxies, and the energies which encompass them. This connection is not limited to our own Milky Way Galaxy, but is inclusive of ALL galaxies, including those in the entirety of the multiverse. In our expanded, present, and grounded state, we are in an empowered state of Love, and we connect to the Galactic Consciousness as it flows within and around us.

The Eternal Divine Being of the Love That You Are is awakened to new levels of potential. You are limitless. You are sublime. You are fully capable and have an unobstructed connection to the higher realms and planes of existence. Light Codes flow freely within and around you always, as you embrace your true form.

Connection to Source

Connection to Source

This Light Code shines Universal, Source Love forth to each of us—in all our forms—as a human being, as a soul, and as the Eternal Child. This Code emanates all of the Divine's acceptance, forgiveness, and compassion, and welcomes us home in nurturing Love.

Self-Actualized Autonomy

Self-Actualized Autonomy

This Light Code holds the infinite frequency of self-actualization and the autonomy that comes with such a state. Our individual responsibility goes beyond our actions, thoughts, beliefs, etc. The sudden realization enters our consciousness and is awakened within the depths of our being: *We hold all of the power to determine every moment of our experience.*

Story: Soul's Choice

Our belief systems affect our ability to manifest in physical form, yet it is a great challenge for us to alter our beliefs. Our minds are easily programmed … once. Reprogramming our original program is more difficult than the installation of the first program. This is why the "New Age" psychological movement of "Belief Work" has become increasingly popular. Add in the science of epigenetics (which has proven the impact that our thoughts and beliefs have on the replication quality of DNA and expression of our genes), and the importance of doing belief work becomes apparent. We are not victims of external circumstances: *We are victims only of ourselves.* We are in control of how we experience life, and how difficult or easy we make our life falls directly to our mindset. We can *fight* with life, or we can *flow* with life. Even through adverse situations, we get to choose how we want to navigate them. This is our free will! Although disease and trauma can occur anytime to anyone (these are the hazards of living on this physical planet), how we experience them is up to us.

You may be wondering, "What about special cases, such as those people who are born into poverty or who are born with a heart-breaking birth defect?" Indeed, these are very challenging and tragic examples. While we grapple with the illusory realities of pain and suffering, we are reminded that through darkness, there is Light. Sometimes, souls will choose a challenging incarnation to maximize their learning potential. From the soul's wide-range vantage and perspective, while blanketed in Love and amazing high vibrations, living on this planet can appear "easy." Sometimes souls take on difficult situations believing it won't be as challenging as it really is.

Even through undeniably difficult challenges, every life is a valuable experience for our soul. It is our soul that chooses every life we live. In other words, your soul chose your exact time, place, parents, and the circumstances surrounding your birth. Your soul chose certain programs and karmic lessons it wanted to explore and complete. Some of this is due to your soul's sheer curiosity in wanting to discover, learn, grow, and come to know itself better. Some circumstances are karmic, others are based on soul-to-soul contracts and agreements, still others are based purely on the soular wound, and the attraction of energies surrounding the wound.

Even if we take on an energetic or physically intense life, there is still the possibility that we can transmute (release) vast amounts of energy that the soul is ready to heal and release. There is also the possibility that the soul wanted to take on a challenge in order to try something new or to work with something in a different way than perhaps was experienced in a previous life. The soul might say "That didn't work … let's try it this way …. "

In coming to know itself better, the soul has the opportunity to rediscover and feel certain feelings again. For example, the soul enjoys experiencing romantic love for the first time. The soul loves learning new skills, gaining new knowledge, and feeling new sensations. A soul might like to stay in a certain energy for a long time, to maximize its experience until it feels complete with that energy. *This is a good reason not to judge others, because we don't know what their soul is seeking to experience.*

The soul needs to make what we humans call "mistakes," so it can determine if something "was a good idea or not." The soul chooses difficult incarnations because there is much to learn from challenging situations. For example, if an individual is born into a highly dysfunctional body, household, or situation, that soul may be looking to gain valuable experiential information that is only available under those conditions. There might also be a karmic tie to the energies of the situation, which the soul might have a chance to neutralize in this incarnation.

If we are able to work consciously with our particular challenges (whatever they may be), and see from the soul's perspective that a human life is a sacred, focused point of energy manifested into a physical reality, we might be able to take ourselves a little less seriously. Indeed, the physical life *is* sacred—it is for a purpose. We may not understand fully our own unique, individual purpose or the complexities of the agreements, karmic lessons, soul desires, and wounds we have arranged for ourselves … but we can seek to gain a greater perspective of all things.

With this broader lens, we can begin to see how our soular wounds have shaped our lives. We can take ownership of ourselves, our experience, and our existence. We can see why we chose our families, our culture, our programming, even our physical ailments. We can take ownership of our interaction with others and ourselves, and ultimately, when we see our truth with this level of clarity, the veil of illusion lifts. We are no longer victims incarnated on this planet. We have realized the eternal nature of ourselves at our core: We are empowered, fully embodied, fully activated, and in command and in harmony with Universal Love. We take in this Universal Love with every sip of water, every bite of food, and every breath we take. This Love courses through our body every moment of every day, nourishing, healing, and connecting us in ways we never dreamed possible. There is unlimited potential on all levels of our existence.

The soular wound is the key to making connections with our heart, our higher self, our soul, and the truth of our reality. The soular wound belongs to no one but you. It is up to you when you choose to look at it, to feel it, to acknowledge it, and to reframe it. The soular wound is there to be healed, and the more people that make a declaration to heal their own wound and to reclaim their power and inner authority, the easier it will be for others to follow suit. Remember, there is no time—time is an illusion of the physical realm. This means that the wounds of all souls are simultaneously active and completely healed. The question is, which timeline are you going to choose?

A Blessing

Thank you, dear reader, for your bravery, honesty, and Love. We all work together to bring forward new levels of healing to all, but we must start with ourselves. After reading these stories and the wisdom channeled to us by the Beings of Love and Light who support us in our deep awakening and our healing processes, consider that you have received an initiation—an initiation in part into the Golden Age: an age of harmony that resonates with the rhythms and pulses of Universal Love.

Postscript

I hope the messages in this book have brought you comfort, knowledge, and healing in your beautiful and unique life. I encourage you to help others to discover this book and find healing for themselves and humanity by sharing your experience with *Light Codes for the Soul* on Amazon and Goodreads.

To work with Laara, to go deeper into Light Codes, and for questions, suggestions, or media inquiries, please visit us at www.lightcodesbylaara.com

Glossary

◉   **Attractor Field:** the term used to describe our energy body's ability to attract to itself energies similar to it and parallel to those which occupy its own energetic space. ("Like attracts like.")

◉   **Beauty:** an essence derived from Love.

◉   **Download:** a large amount of energetic information given by Spirit to an individual, and integrated deep within the receiver's mind, body, and soul.

◉   **The Divine:** the all-encompassing Light being you resonate with (e.g. Great Spirit, God, Source, Spirit, Universe, etc.).

◉   **Ego:** the limited identity of self in physical form; the lower self.

◉   **Eternal Child:** the innocence of our soul.

◉   **Heart Coherence:** a physiological state of balance between the sympathetic and parasympathetic nervous systems which helps to establish a clear connection between our lower and higher selves.

◉   **Higher Self:** the omniscient Light Being who acts as a connection between the soul and the ego.

◉   **Illusion:** the truth of our holographic reality.

◉   **Incoherence:** the physiological imbalance of the nervous system and of thought, and the ultimate disconnection between the lower and higher selves.

⊚ **Love:** Love is God, God is Love. It is the natural law of the universe of truth.

⊚ **Mind:** the thinking brain, directed by our ego.

⊚ **Negative Energy Space:** low, stagnant, or incoherent vibrational energies.

⊚ **Positive Energy Space:** coherent, flowing, and light vibrational energies.

⊚ **Soul:** the infinite energetic "real" you, fully connected to Source and the Love That You Are.

⊚ **Universal Law:** the laws that Love governs.

⊚ **Upgrade:** the ultimate outcome of a download.

References

Dispenza, Joe. *Becoming Supernatural: How Common People are Doing the Uncommon*. Carlsbad: Hay House, 2017.

Green, Glenda. *Love Without End – Jesus Speaks*. Sedona: Spiritus, 1999.

HeartMath® Institute. www.heartmath.org

Laara. *The Little Book of Light Codes: Healing Symbols for Life Transformation*. Victoria: Peacock Wisdom Publishing, 2020.

Laara. *Fractalline Healing*™. Victoria: Peacock Wisdom Publishing. (Coming in 2021.)

Lipton, Bruce H. *The Biology of Belief: Unleashing the Power of Consciousness, Matter & Miracles*. Carlsbad: Hay House, 2011.

Suggested Reading List

Bruyere, Rosalyn L. *Wheels of Light: Chakras, Auras, and the Healing Energy of the Body*. New York: Fireside, 1994.

Dispenza, Joe. *Becoming Supernatural: How Common People are Doing the Uncommon*. Carlsbad: Hay House, 2017.

Green, Glenda. *Love Without End – Jesus Speaks*. Sedona: Spiritus, 1999.

Laara. *Fractalline Healing*™. Victoria: Peacock Wisdom Publishing. (Coming in 2021.)

Laara. *The Little Book of Light Codes: Healing Symbols for Life Transformation*. Victoria: Peacock Wisdom Publishing, 2020.

Lipton, Bruce H. *The Biology of Belief: Unleashing the Power of Consciousness, Matter & Miracles*. Carlsbad: Hay House, 2011.

Miller, Lisa M. *The Heart of Leadership for Women: Cultivating a Sacred Space*. Bloomington: Balboa Press, 2020.

Reynolds, Kay. *The Evidential Medium: A Practical Guide for Developing Mediumship*. Mind Blown Press, 2020.

Ruiz, Don Miguel and Janet Mills. *The Four Agreements: A Toltec Wisdom Book*. San Rafael: Amber-Allen Publishing Inc., 1997.

Schucman, Helen. *A Course in Miracles: Combined Volume*. Mill Valley: Foundation for Inner Peace, 2007.

More information about Fractalline Healing™ can be found at www.fractallinehealing.com

About the Author

Laara, Tigress of the Light, is a healing practitioner, channeler, and intuitive. Before focusing on energy and healing, for twenty years she competed up to an international level in the equestrian sport of show jumping. Now she practices a variety of healing modalities and continues to learn from acclaimed healer and teacher, Rosalyn L. Bruyere and other cherished mentors. Laara enjoys practicing yoga, riding her horses, and living an ever-evolving, healthy, and balanced lifestyle. Laara lives in Victoria, B.C. Canada. You can connect with her at: LightCodesByLaara.com

Notes

Notes

Notes

Notes

Notes

Notes

Notes

Notes